The Heinemann Illustrated Encyclopedia

Volume 2

Bis-Cor

First published in Great Britain by Heinemann Library
Halley Court, Jordan Hill, Oxford OX2 8EJ
a division of Reed Educational and Professional Publishing Ltd.

OXFORD MELBOURNE AUCKLAND
JOHANNESBURG BLANTYRE GABORONE
IBADAN PORTSMOUTH NH (USA) CHICAGO

Series Editors: Rebecca and Stephen Vickers
Author Team: Rob Alcraft, Catherine Chambers, Jim Drake,
Fred Martin, Angela Royston, Jane Shuter, Roger Thomas,
Rebecca Vickers, Stephen Vickers
Reading Consultant: Betty Root

Photo research by Katharine Smith
Designed and Typeset by Gecko Ltd
Printed in Hong Kong by Wing King Tong

02 01 00 99 98
10 9 8 7 6 5 4 3 2 1

ISBN 0 431 09053 X

British Library Cataloguing in Publication Data.

The Heinemann illustrated encyclopedia
1. Children's encyclopedias and dictionaries
I. Vickers, Rebecca II. Vickers, Stephen, 1951–
032

ISBN 0431090629

Acknowledgements:
Cover: The cover illustration is of a male specimen of *Ornithoptera goliath*, commonly called the
Goliath Birdwing. Special thanks to Dr George C. McGavin and the Hope Entomological
Collections, Oxford University Museum of Natural History.

Ancient Art and Architecture: p11. **Aquarius:** 21b. **Clive Barda:** p38. **BBC Natural History
Unit:** Duncan McEwan – p27b. **Dave Bradford:** p26t. **J. Allan Cash Ltd.:** pp6, 7, 8, 10, 12t, 14,
19, 22, 31, 34, 35, 43b. **Bruce Coleman:** Werner Layer – p26b. **Empics:** Rachel Crosbie – p23b.
Fox and Shaw Design Consultants: p18. **Chris Honeywell:** p29b. **Hulton Getty:** p24t.
The Hutchison Library: pp12b, 24b, 37; Jeremy A. Horner – p42. **Image Bank:** Gary Gladstone
– p45t. **Medimage:** Antony King – p46. **Oxford Scientific Films:** Animal, Animal – p4b (Lynn M.
Stone); Kate Atkinson – p41b; G.I. Bernard – p41t David Breed – p32b; Cooke – p33b; Jack Dermid
– p17r; Bob Fredrick – p16b; Mickey Gibson – p20t; Mark Hamblin – p40b; Breck P. Kent – p27t;
Okapia – p13b; Stan Osolinski – p4t; Peter Parks – pp30, 48; Norbet Rosing – p32t; Jim Tuten –
p20b; David Wright - p29t. **Royal Geographical Society:** p40t. **Science Photo Library:**
James King-Holmes – p5b; Jerry Lodriguss – p44t; Pekka Parvianen – p44b. **ZEFA:** p36;
Gerolf Kalt – 15b.

Every effort has been made to contact copyright holders of any material
reproduced in this book. Any omissions will be rectified in subsequent printings if
notice is given to the Publisher

Welcome to the
Heinemann Illustrated Encyclopedia

What is an encyclopedia?

An encyclopedia is an information book. It gives the most important facts about a lot of different subjects. This encyclopedia has been specially written for children your age. It covers many of the subjects from school and others you may find interesting.

What is in this encyclopedia?

In this encyclopedia each topic is called an entry. There is one page for every entry. The entries in this encyclopedia are on:

- animals
- plants
- dinosaurs
- countries
- geography
- history
- world religions
- music
- art
- transport
- science
- technology

How to use this encyclopedia

This encyclopedia has eleven books, called volumes. The first ten volumes contain entries. The entries are all in alphabetical order. This means that Volume One starts with entries that begin with the letter 'A' and Volume Ten ends with entries that begin with the letter 'Z'. Volume Eleven is the index volume and has some other interesting information in its Fact Finder section.

Here are two entries, showing you what you can find on a page:

The See also line tells you where to find other related information.

This is the letter that the entry starts with.

Fact boxes give you details about the topic.

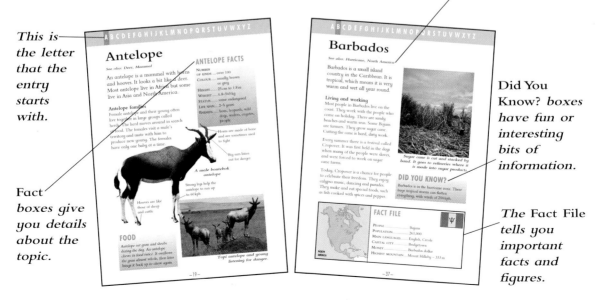

Did You Know? boxes have fun or interesting bits of information.

The Fact File tells you important facts and figures.

Bison

See also: Buffalo, Mammal

Bison are a type of long-haired wild cattle. They are mammals. The wisent, or European bison, lives mostly in Poland. The American bison lives in Canada and the USA. Only 150 years ago there were 60 million American bison. Hunters have killed so many that now there are fewer than 100,000.

Bison families

A male bison is called a bull and a female bison is called a cow. The cow has a calf every year. Most bulls, cows and calves live together in large groups called herds. When there is danger, the bulls make a circle around the cows and calves.

Bison move from place to place looking for food, so their home is wherever they are feeding.

FOOD

Bison eat grass and drink water. Before most land was fenced in, bison used to walk north in the spring to find new grass, and go south in the autumn.

BISON FACTS

NUMBER OF KINDS	2
COLOUR	brown
HEIGHT	1.5–2 m
WEIGHT	up to 1000 kg
STATUS	threatened
LIFE SPAN	around 20 years
ENEMIES	wolves, coyotes

Hunters used to kill bison.

Wool-like coat keeps it warm in winter

Horns are used for fighting

Good sense of smell to avoid danger

Hooves that spread out are good for walking on grass and snow

An American bison bull

This American bison calf is being guarded from danger.

Blood

See also: Heart, Human body

Blood is a liquid that moves around the bodies of most animals. The heart pumps it along pipes called arteries. Other pipes, called veins, carry the blood back to the heart.

What is blood?

Blood is made up mostly of water with tiny cells in it. There are millions of cells in every drop of blood. Most are red cells, which carry oxygen and give blood its colour. A few are white cells that fight disease.

What is blood for?

Blood carries food to the brain and muscles. Oxygen from the lungs is carried in the blood to all parts of the body. Blood also carries away any waste. Blood can help the body to cool by moving to just under the skin. This makes the skin look red.

New blood

If someone loses a lot of blood quickly, the body may not be able to replace it. This can cause illness or death. Doctors can help by giving a blood transfusion into the sick person's veins.

FACTS

A growing child's body usually has about five litres of blood.

Heart

Lungs put oxygen in the blood

Arteries

Veins

This shows blood moving around the human body. The red blood has oxygen in it. The blue blood is going back to the lungs.

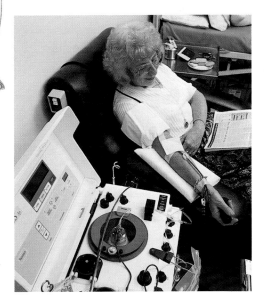

This woman is giving blood. Blood donors give blood so that hospitals can keep a store of blood ready for emergencies.

Bolivia

See also: South America

Bolivia is a country in South America. In the west there is high, flat land and the Andes Mountains. In the east is the low, hot jungle of the Amazon.

Living and working

Most Bolivians are farmers. The whole family works together to grow crops such as potatoes and maize. They build small, one-storey houses from mud bricks. When children are not at school they look after the animals, which are usually llamas and sheep. Bolivians in the countryside weave clothes of brilliant colours. Many native women wear hard, round-topped hats. They look a bit like big bowler hats.

The potato comes from Bolivia. People in the mountain regions of the country eat them all year. They trample them, to squeeze out the water. Then they freeze the potatoes in the cold mountain air.

Local women wear hats and shawls to the market at Tihuanaca.

DID YOU KNOW?

Lake Titicaca in Bolivia is the highest lake in the world.

SOUTH AMERICA

FACT FILE

PEOPLE .... Bolivians

POPULATION .... 7.9 million

MAIN LANGUAGES .... Spanish, Aymara, Quéchua

CAPITAL CITY .... La Paz

MONEY .... Boliviano

HIGHEST MOUNTAIN ... Sajama – 6542 m

LONGEST RIVER .... River Madeira – 3380 km

Bosnia-Hercegovina

See also: Europe, Yugoslavia

Bosnia-Hercegovina is in south-east Europe. It has many mountains with forests growing on them. The north is flat and has cold, snowy winters and warm, wet summers. The south has mild winters and hot summers.

Living and working

Many people in Bosnia-Hercegovina live in small towns and villages. Traditional houses are often made of grey stone with grey or red tiled roofs. Some people make woollen rugs and silk fabrics in bright patterns. In the countryside, farmers grow cereals, fruit, berries and nuts.

For breakfast some Bosnians eat *burek*. This is a pie layered with cheese, meat or potato. A favourite sweet is *baclava*, a sticky pastry filled with nuts, dried fruit and honey.

Local market traders get ready to set up in the Bacarsija Tower Square in Sarajevo.

DID YOU KNOW?

Some Bosnians write the Serbo-Croat language using the Roman alphabet – like this book. Others use the Cyrillic alphabet, which has some different letter-shapes for the sounds.

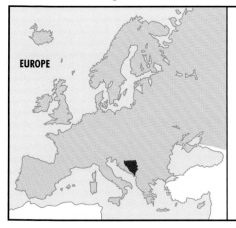

EUROPE

FACT FILE

PEOPLE........................Bosnians

POPULATION...............4.3 million

MAIN LANGUAGE........ Serbo-Croat

CAPITAL CITY..............Sarajevo

MONEY........................Dinar

HIGHEST MOUNTAIN....Mount Maglic – 2386 m

LONGEST RIVER...........River Bosna – 250 km

Botswana

See also: Africa

Botswana is in southern Africa. Most of the country is flat. There are marshlands and farms in the north. Part of the Kalahari Desert is in the south-west. It is mostly hot and dry, with a little rain.

Some of the houses in this village are traditional round buildings with cone-shaped thatched roofs.

Living and working

Most people in Botswana live in small towns and large villages. Many houses are made from sun-baked bricks, with corrugated iron roofs. People in Botswana eat a kind of porridge made with corn, sorghum or millet. This is usually served with fish, bean and vegetable stews.

Farmers grow corn, sorghum, millet and beans. Mining is an important industry. There are not enough jobs for everyone in Botswana, so many people leave to find work in South Africa.

DID YOU KNOW?

The San people of the Kalahari Desert are famous for making drinking flasks out of ostrich eggs.

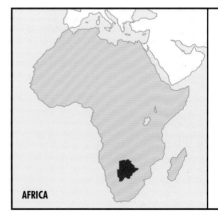

AFRICA

FACT FILE

PEOPLE .... Botswanans

POPULATION .... nearly 1.5 million

MAIN LANGUAGES .... English, Setswana

CAPITAL CITY .... Gaborone

MONEY .... Pula

HIGHEST MOUNTAIN .... Tsodilo Hill – 1300 m

LONGEST RIVER .... River Botletle – 370 km

Brachiosaur

See also: Dinosaur, Fossil

The brachiosaur was a giant four-legged dinosaur. It was one of the largest and longest dinosaurs. It weighed as much as six elephants. With its long neck it was as tall as a four-storey building.

Life style

The brachiosaur lived 113 to 150 million years ago. It was a peaceful giant. It plodded slowly through forests and lived in small groups or herds. The brachiosaur was so large it had to spend most of its time eating.

BRACHIOSAUR FACTS

COLOUR	not known
HEIGHT	12 m
LENGTH	25 m
WEIGHT	30–50 tonnes
LIFE SPAN	They may have taken a hundred years just to grow into adults.
ENEMIES	It was so big it had few or no enemies.

Sharp chisel teeth to cut through tough plants

Long neck for reaching treetop leaves

Massive bones to hold up tall body and huge weight

Long tail to balance heavy body and long neck

Sharp claws may have been used to fight

The brachiosaur

FOOD

The brachiosaur probably ate mostly leaves. It could not chew. It needed to swallow stones from time to time to help grind up food in its stomach.

Brazil

See also: Rainforest, South America

Brazil is the largest country in South America. In the north is the Amazon River and the world's largest rainforest. It is always hot and wet there.

Living and working

Most Brazilians live in modern cities near the coasts. There are tall concrete buildings and factories. Many city people live in poor, small houses. Most towns and cities have busy markets. People sell food, such as roasted maize and watermelons.

In the north-east farmers grow maize. Some native people still live in the rainforest. They hunt, fish and collect plants for food.

Every February in the city of Rio de Janeiro, there is a festival called Carnival. There are parades. People wear fantastic costumes and dance the samba.

Rubber is collected from trees in Brazil. Many rubber-trappers live in forest huts like these.

DID YOU KNOW?

The Amazon rainforest of Brazil is home to one quarter of all the different kinds of plants and animals in the world.

SOUTH AMERICA

FACT FILE

PEOPLE .... Brazilians
POPULATION .... 159.5 million
MAIN LANGUAGE .... Portuguese
CAPITAL CITY .... Brasília
LARGEST CITY .... São Paulo
MONEY .... Real
HIGHEST MOUNTAIN .... Pico da Neblina – 3014 m
LONGEST RIVER .... Amazon – 6500 km

Bronze Age

See also: Iron Age, Stone Age

The Bronze Age is the time in an area's history when people made tools and weapons from bronze instead of stone. Bronze is a metal made of a mixture of copper and tin.

When was the Bronze Age?

Different peoples discovered how to make weapons and tools from bronze at different times. Even in the same country, people did not all start using bronze at the same time. First they had to learn how to make and work with bronze.

Why was bronze important?

Tools and weapons made with bronze were sharper and better than those made with stone. Bronze could be made into many kinds of shapes when it was still hot. It could even be melted to a liquid and poured into moulds. It was much easier to work with than stone.

However, there was not much copper in the ground for people to dig up to make bronze. In many places, people could not get any at all. People looked for a new metal to use instead. By 1000 BC, iron was being used.

KEY DATES

6000 BC .. People in the Middle East begin to use copper

3500 BC .. People in the Middle East begin to use bronze

2500 BC .. People in India begin to use bronze

2500 BC .. People in Europe begin to use bronze

1600 BC .. People in China begin to use bronze

1000 BC .. People in Greece begin to use iron

Bronze was used to make jewellery and pins to fasten clothes. This torc is a thick bronze ring to go around a person's arm or neck. Only wealthy men and women wore them.

Buddhism

See also: India

Buddhism is a world religion. People who follow this religion are called Buddhists. Buddhism grew from the teachings of Prince Siddhartha Gautama. He is known as the Buddha. This means 'the Enlightened One' – the one who found truth.

Beliefs and teachings

The Buddha was born over 2500 years ago in Nepal. Even though he was a prince, the Buddha gave up all his riches. He became a travelling preacher.

The Buddha's teachings are written down in a book called the Tripitaka. Buddhist monks and other Buddhist followers study these writings. They aim to be kind and peaceful and always do the right thing.

Buddhism today

There are now about 300 million Buddhists all over the world. Most live in Asia. Buddhists pray and meditate at home or in temples. They also make offerings of fruit, flowers and incense. An important festival is the Buddha's birthday.

This man is praying in front of a statue of the Buddha in a Buddhist temple. The statue is surrounded by flowers and other offerings.

This is the Buddhist Wheel of Life. It shows life, death and rebirth.

Buffalo

See also: Bison, Mammal

Buffalo are a very strong type of wild cattle. They are mammals. There are three main kinds of buffalo. These are the Southern Asian and European water buffalo, the African cape buffalo and the forest buffalo. The forest buffalo is the smallest and has the shortest horns. Farmers keep buffalo to pull ploughs and for other work.

Buffalo families

A male buffalo is called a bull and a female buffalo is called a cow. The cow has one calf, every year. In the wild, cows, calves and a few strong bulls live together in a large group, called a herd.

BUFFALO FACTS

NUMBER OF KINDS	3
COLOUR	mainly grey, but the forest buffalo is reddish-brown
HEIGHT	1.3–1.7 m
WEIGHT	up to 900 kg
STATUS	threatened
LIFE SPAN	around 18 years
ENEMIES	crocodiles, lions, people

Horns help the bulls to fight

Thick hide gives protection against thorns

A water buffalo bull

Hooves spread out for walking and running on grass and mud

FOOD

Buffalo eat grass and leaves and drink lots of water. They eat in the evenings and rest during the day.

This herd of wild water buffalo is grazing in Sri Lanka.

Bulgaria

See also: Europe

Bulgaria is a country in south-east Europe. Mountains and hills cover half of it. Summers are mostly hot and dry. Winters are cold. It is warmer and wetter in the south-west.

Living and working

Over half the population of Bulgaria lives in cities and towns. Some old stone houses have wooden beams, balconies and open porches. People in Bulgaria eat a lot of sheep's cheese and yoghurt. They also like meat stuffed with mushrooms, cheese and sausage.

Farmers grow cereals, cotton, flowers, tobacco and grapes. There are mines and factories.

Tourists visit Bulgaria all year round. In the summer they go to the resorts on the Black Sea. In the winter they ski in the mountains.

The government buildings are in the capital Sofia. They face on to a large public, central square.

DID YOU KNOW?

Bulgaria makes most of the world's rose oil. It is used in perfume, tea and syrup. It takes 2000 rose petals to make one gram of oil.

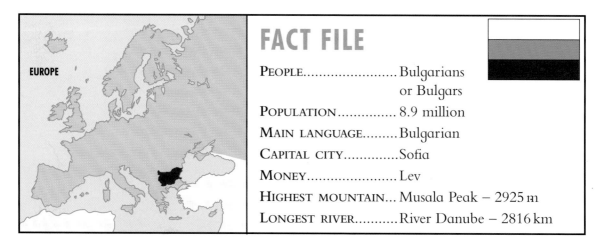

EUROPE

FACT FILE

PEOPLE	Bulgarians or Bulgars
POPULATION	8.9 million
MAIN LANGUAGE	Bulgarian
CAPITAL CITY	Sofia
MONEY	Lev
HIGHEST MOUNTAIN	Musala Peak – 2925 m
LONGEST RIVER	River Danube – 2816 km

Bus

See also: Transport

A bus is a large vehicle used for transporting people. The first buses were built hundreds of years ago.

The first buses

Buses were needed as cities and towns grew larger. They could carry people quickly and cheaply from where they lived, to where they worked. The first buses were pulled by horses. Some buses ran on rails. They were known as trams.

BUS FIRSTS

FIRST INVENTED	France, 1662
FIRST PUBLIC BUS SERVICE	Paris, 1662
FIRST MOTOR BUS	Germany, 1895

An early double-decker bus in London. The first buses were pulled by horses.

How buses are used

Buses can carry many passengers. They do not take up much more road space than a car. In cities they are quick and efficient. Because there are buses, fewer people have to travel into the city in their own cars. In some cities there are double-decker buses that can carry nearly twice as many people as a single-decker bus. In countries where people cannot afford cars, buses are the only way to travel long distances.

Greyhound buses are famous in the United States. They carry passengers between every major town and city.

Butterfly

See also: Caterpillar, Metamorphosis

Butterflies are insects with coloured wings. They are found almost all over the world. Some butterflies live their whole lives in one place. Others migrate long distances to escape cold winters.

BUTTERFLY FACTS

NUMBER OF KINDS	15,000–20,000
COLOUR	many different colours and patterns
WINGSPAN	1–8 cm
STATUS	some types are endangered
LIFE SPAN	from a few months to more than a year
ENEMIES	birds

Butterfly families

A butterfly begins life as an egg which hatches into a caterpillar. When the caterpillar is fully grown, it becomes a pupa. Inside the hard shell of the pupa, the caterpillar changes into a butterfly. After a while, the adult butterfly breaks out of the shell.

Each butterfly lives mainly on its own, flying from flower to flower to find food. Butterflies only come together to mate and to migrate.

Antennae to smell food and help find a mate

Wings made of tiny scales which may form colourful patterns

A goliath birdwinged butterfly

FOOD

A butterfly unrolls its long tongue and uses it to suck the sugary juice made by flowers. The juice is called nectar.

This pupa of a purple emperor butterfly is attached to a leaf while it develops into an adult butterfly.

Cactus

See also: Desert, Plant

A cactus is a plant with a prickly stem and no leaves. Most cacti grow in hot deserts in North and South America.

The life of a cactus

Cacti grow in very dry places. Flowers grow at the top and sides of the stem and make fruits full of seeds. The seeds fall to the ground. Some of them will grow into cacti the next time it rains.

Birds, small animals and insects feed on the flowers and stems of cacti. Birds nest among their spines. People eat the fruit and seeds of some cacti. Cacti are often kept as house plants.

CACTUS FACTS

NUMBER OF KINDS	2000
HEIGHT	2 cm to 18 m
LIFE SPAN	up to 200 years
ENEMIES	desert animals and people

The saguaro is the tallest cactus. Its huge arms reach high above the desert in Arizona.

Bright flowers attract insects

Sharp spines stop animals eating the juicy stem

Thick, waxy skin keeps the water in

A barrel cactus in flower.

Calendar

See also: Season, Time

A calendar is a way to measure time. The Earth and moon move. This helps to measure how time passes.

Years

For a long time, calendars have shown years divided into about 365 days. This is the amount of time it takes for the Earth to go around the sun once. Using a calendar like this, the seasons come in the same months every year.

Some calendars have patterns for their years. The Chinese have a pattern of twelve year names that are repeated. Each of the twelve years is named after an animal – such as a rat or a monkey.

Months and weeks

Many calendars divide the year up into months of about 30 days, which is how long it takes for the moon to go once around the Earth.

Most calendars now have weeks that last seven days. This comes from the Bible, which says that people should rest on every seventh day, instead of working.

DID YOU KNOW?

Every four years an extra day is added to the calendar. That day is always the 29th of February. A year with the extra day is called a leap year.

September

September

11 **ETHIOPIAN NEW YEAR'S DAY**
Rastafarians celebrate the New Year.

11 ~ 20 **PARYUSHANA PARVA**
Eight to ten days festival in which Jains emulate the lifestyle of their leaders.

21 ~ 30 **NAVARATRI/DURGA PUJA**
Hindus celebrate a festival of nine nights of worship of the goddess Durga, the Hindus' most important female deity.

21 ~ 22 **ROSH HASHANA**
Jewish New Year's Day.

27 **HARVEST FESTIVAL**
Celebrated at autumn time. Foodstuffs are collected and often distributed to the aged and those in need.

30 **YOM KIPPUR**
Jewish people commemorate the last day of the ten days of repentance. This is the Day of Atonement and the holiest day of the year. A day of fasting.

This is the month of September on a multi-faith calendar. It lists the holidays and festivals of countries and different religions.

Cambodia

See also: Asia

Cambodia is a country in south-east Asia. There are hills and mountains to the north, east and south-west. The climate is hot and wet, with some flooding.

The Royal Palace in Phnom Penh has many overlapping roofs. It has beautiful gardens.

Living and working

Most people in Cambodia live in the countryside. Near the Mekong River there are floating homes and also houses built on stilts. People in Cambodia eat a lot of fish and meat with rice. They sometimes add ginger, lemongrass or sesame oil to give the food a different flavour.

Farmers grow rice, cassava, soybeans, sesame and tropical fruits. People mine for jewels and work in factories.

DID YOU KNOW?

Cambodian craftworkers weave cloth into traditional patterns and pictures of animals. They use thread made from real gold and silver.

ASIA

FACT FILE

PEOPLE	Cambodians, Khmer
POPULATION	10.8 million
MAIN LANGUAGE	Khmer
CAPITAL CITY	Phnom Penh
MONEY	New riel
HIGHEST MOUNTAIN	Kompong Chhnang – 1813 m
LONGEST RIVER	Mekong River – 4506 km

Camel

See also: Desert, Mammal

Camels are large mammals that live in the deserts of Africa, Asia and Australia. Arabian camels have one hump and Bactrian camels, which live in parts of Asia, have two humps. There are still some wild camels, but most camels are used by people to carry things and to ride on.

Camel families

A male camel is called a bull and a female is called a cow. The cow gives birth to one baby at a time. It is called a calf or a foal. Wild camels live together in a group, called a herd. They wander around looking for food.

CAMEL FACTS

NUMBER OF KINDS ...	2
COLOUR	brown
SHOULDER HEIGHT ...	up to 2 m
WEIGHT	250–680 kg
STATUS	wild camels are endangered
LIFE SPAN..................	up to 40 years

Large fatty hump stores energy to use when food is short

Hairs inside and outside ears keep out the sand

Long lashes keep sand out of the eyes

An Arabian camel

Long, strong legs help the camel to carry heavy loads

Toes spread out to stop the camel sinking into the sand

A female Arabian camel grazing with her newborn calf.

FOOD

Camels eat desert plants, including dates, grasses and thorny bushes. A camel can survive for many weeks without eating or drinking water. When it does drink, it has up to 200 litres a day.

Camera

See also: Light, Television

A camera is a machine that can store a picture on plastic film or on a computer disk. Some cameras take still pictures called photographs. Other cameras, such as movie and video cameras, can take moving pictures.

Catching the image

Every camera has a lens made of see-through glass or plastic. The lens bends light to make a clear image on the film. When the button on the camera is pressed, a cover called a shutter opens to let light in. The shutter closes again very quickly. In a still camera the image is made on thin plastic film. TV and video cameras use special CCD microchips to take the pictures. Digital cameras store the image as information on a disk.

shutter speed locator

rewind lever

A roll of film

lenses

shutter

A camera

Moving pictures

A movie camera is like a still camera. It takes pictures called frames. It takes 24 frames every second. The film moves after each frame is taken. This gives a line of pictures. The frames are shown (projected) one after another. The brain thinks it is seeing smooth movement.

This television programme is being filmed outside. Tracks have been laid so that the camera can be moved smoothly as it films.

Canada

See also: Native Americans, North America

Canada is a country in North America. There are mountains in the east and west. There are many islands in the north. It is cold in the winter and hot in the summer, except in the north where it never gets very warm. Canada is the second biggest country in the world.

Living and working

Most people live in the south. Some people live in modern cities, but others live in towns villages and farms. The big areas of flat land are used for growing cereals, tobacco and flax. The land is also good for grazing. The huge forests of Canada supply wood which is used for many things, including paper.

The first people in Canada were the ancestors of Native Americans who arrived around 40,000 years ago. Later the Inuit peoples moved from Asia into northern areas of Canada.

The Athabasca glacier is in Jasper National Park.

DID YOU KNOW?

Canadian police who ride horses are called 'Mounties'. This comes from their full name, which is the Royal Canadian Mounted Police.

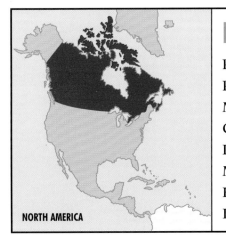

NORTH AMERICA

FACT FILE

PEOPLE	Canadians
POPULATION	28.8 million
MAIN LANGUAGES	English, French
CAPITAL CITY	Ottawa
LARGEST CITY	Toronto
MONEY	Canadian dollar
HIGHEST MOUNTAIN	Mount Logan – 6050 m
LONGEST RIVER	Mackenzie River – 3782 km

Canoe

See also: Native Americans, Transport

A canoe is a small boat that is pushed through the water with paddles. Canoes are one of the oldest kinds of boat in the world.

CANOE FIRSTS

FIRST INVENTED	at least 10,000 years ago
FIRST CANOE CLUB	England, 1866
FIRST OLYMPIC CANOE COMPETITION....	Berlin, 1936

The first canoes

The first canoes were made from hollowed-out tree trunks. They are called dug-outs. Canoes like these are still used all over the world for transporting goods or people. Sometimes they have small sails.

Native Americans built canoes from the bark of trees. The Inuit people of the Arctic built canoes using a wooden frame covered with sealskin.

This Native American canoe is made of birch bark attached to a wooden frame.

How canoes are used

In most countries canoes are now used for sport and leisure, not for transport. Open canoes (Canadian canoes) and one- and two-seat closed canoes (kayaks) are used in competitions which test speed and skills. There are six canoe events in the Olympic Games.

This canoeist is competing in the 1996 Olympic Games in Atlanta, Georgia, USA.

Car

See also: Engine, Transport

A car is a vehicle with three or four wheels and an engine. There are seats inside for a driver and passengers. Cars move using the energy from the engine.

The first cars

Cars were invented in 1885. At first, cars were slow, unreliable and very expensive. Not many people used them.

Then, in America, Henry Ford began to build small cars, called 'Model Ts', that ordinary people could afford. The cars had a top speed of 65 kph. Since then, better engines have made cars more reliable and able to go faster. Today there are so many cars on the roads that they make problems such as traffic jams and air pollution.

How cars are used

In many countries, nearly every family owns a car to make travelling easy and quick. Having cars means that people can work and shop a long way from where they live.

Cars are useful, but too many can cause problems. This traffic jam is on the Golden Gate Bridge in San Francisco in California, USA.

CAR FIRSTS

FIRST INVENTED	1885
FIRST FORD MODEL T	1908
FASTEST	*Thrust,* 1,226 kph

The driver and passengers in this early 1900s car are wearing goggles to protect their eyes from dust and grit.

Castle

See also: Knight, Middle Ages

A castle is a building surrounded by walls, designed to keep out enemies. Castles were built for kings and other important people. The way castles were built changed because the weapons used against them changed.

KEY DATES

1050...Castles were made out of wood

1150...Stone castles were built with high walls

1340...Small cannons were used in battles

1400...Big cannons were used in battles

1480...Stone castles were built with lower walls

This cutaway drawing is an artist's idea of what a small castle in the Middle Ages would have looked like when it was first built. Most of the stairways were spiral.

The first castles

The first castles were made of wood. Many were motte and bailey castles. This kind of castle had a tower built on a hill with a wall around it – the motte. The motte was inside a bigger, flatter area that also had a wall around it – the bailey. Almost all castles had at least one deep ditch around the outside of the walls. Sometimes the ditch was filled with water. This is called a moat.

Later castles

Later castles were made of stone. They still used the idea of a tower inside walls. The first stone castles had high walls. Then cannons were invented. Cannons shot big, heavy iron balls at these walls. High, thin walls were easily broken down. People then began to build castles with walls that were not so high, but were much thicker. It was harder to break them with cannon balls.

Cat

See also: Leopard, Lion, Tiger

A cat is a mammal. Animals as large as lions and tigers and as small as pet cats are all members of the cat family. Pet, or domestic, cats are kept all over the world.

Domestic cat families

A male domestic cat is called a tom and the female is sometimes called a queen. Young cats are called kittens. Three to five kittens are usually born at the same time. When a kitten is about ten weeks old, it is ready to go to a new owner and a new home.

DOMESTIC CAT FACTS

NUMBER OF BREEDS	40
COLOUR	black, white, grey, orange or mixtures of these
HEIGHT	usually 20–25 cm
WEIGHT	from 3 to 7 kg
STATUS	common
LIFE SPAN	12–18 years
ENEMIES	dogs

A domestic pet cat

Long tail helps balance

Fur for keeping warm

Large ears that turn to hear sounds

Eyes that see in the dark

Long whiskers to feel its way in the dark

Sharp claws for climbing, fighting and catching food

FOOD

Wild members of the cat family hunt at night. They look for mice and birds. Even when pet cats get plenty of cat food at home, they still like to hunt.

Wildcats still live in some parts of the world. They are the ancestors of pet cats.

Caterpillar

See also: Butterfly, Metamorphosis, Moth

A caterpillar is a stage in the life of a butterfly or moth, so caterpillars are insects. They are found all over the world, in all the places where there are butterflies or moths.

Caterpillar families

A caterpillar begins life as an egg laid by a butterfly or moth. The eggs are laid where there is plenty of food. When the caterpillar hatches it eats and grows. When it is fully grown, it becomes a pupa, then changes into an adult butterfly or moth.

CATERPILLAR FACTS

NUMBER OF KINDS	200,000
COLOUR	green, brown or brightly patterned
LENGTH	5 mm to 15.5 cm
STATUS	common
LIFE SPAN	usually a few weeks before forming a pupa
ENEMIES	birds, other insects, people

Antennae to feel and smell

Strong mouth to chew through plants

Tiny hooks at the end of legs for holding onto leaves

The body has 14 parts, called 'segments'

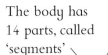

A monarch caterpillar

FOOD

A caterpillar eats more than its own weight in leaves every day. Many caterpillars feed on only one or two kinds of leaves.

When a moth caterpillar is fully grown, it spins a cocoon around itself. Inside the cocoon the caterpillar changes into a moth.

Cathedral

See also: Christianity, Middle Ages

A cathedral is an important Christian church. Most large towns and cities have cathedrals and many people visit them to worship.

Early cathedrals

Most cathedrals were built in the Middle Ages. They were big, impressive buildings and showed how important religion was to people at that time. Cathedrals were built from heavy blocks of stone. They were beautifully carved and painted, inside and out. Some builders worked on the same cathedral their whole lives. Cathedral windows were filled with coloured glass made into beautiful shapes and pictures. These are called stained glass windows.

Later cathedrals

After the Middle Ages, Christians built cathedrals in places all over the world. Some cathedrals, like Coventry Cathedral in England, were built to replace older ones that had been destroyed during World War II.

KEY DATES

FROM 1100...	First stone cathedrals built in Europe
1200–1300...	Many cathedrals were built.
1666.............	St Paul's Cathedral was rebuilt after it burnt down in the Great Fire of London
1800–1900...	Many cathedrals were built in new cities in North America, Australia and across the world
1950–5.........	Coventry Cathedral was rebuilt after it was bombed in World War II
1980.............	The Crystal Cathedral opened in California, USA
1980s...........	In the Central African Republic, a new cathedral was built with the largest dome in the world

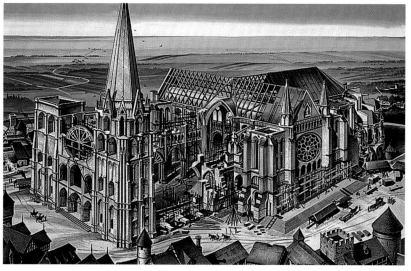

This is an artist's picture of what a medieval cathedral would have looked like at the time it was being built. The builders used very simple tools to make a very large building.

Cattle

See also: Farming, Mammal

Cattle are mammals. They are closely related to buffalo and bison. Wherever there is grass for grazing, farmers rear cattle for meat, milk and hides. Cattle have been raised by farmers for thousands of years.

CATTLE FACTS

NUMBER OF BREEDS	277
COLOUR	usually grey, white, brown, beige, or black
LENGTH	1.6–2.2 m
WEIGHT	up to 2000 kg
STATUS	common
LIFE SPAN	about 20 years
ENEMIES	wolves

Cattle families

The male is called a bull and the female is called a cow. A female usually has one baby, called a calf. Wild cattle live in big groups, called herds. Farmers keep cattle in female-only herds. Because bulls can be very fierce, they are usually kept on their own.

Farmers usually take calves away from their mothers when they are able to feed themselves. They go into their own herd.

A Fresian bull

Tail to swish away insects

Hooves spread out for walking on mud

Four stomachs to help digest tough grass

FOOD

Cattle eat grass. In cold winters, farmers feed cattle with hay and 'cattle cake', made of cereals and vitamins.

This cow is being attached to an automatic milking machine on a modern dairy farm. Cows are milked twice a day.

Centipede

See also: Invertebrate

A centipede is a small animal that looks like a worm with many legs. The name 'centipede' means 'a hundred feet', but centipedes can have from 30 to 350 legs. Centipedes are invertebrates. They are found all over the world. A centipede's bite can be painful or even dangerous to people.

CENTIPEDE FACTS

NUMBER OF KINDS	2800
COLOUR	brown, red, yellow, grey
LENGTH	0.5–30 cm
STATUS	common
LIFE SPAN	7–10 years
ENEMIES	birds, ants

An Australian giant centipede

Each segment of the body has two legs

Antennae feel and smell

Poisonous fangs to kill food

Centipede families

Some female centipedes may lay many eggs at a time. The female curls her body around the eggs to protect them until they hatch. Other kinds of centipede lay just one egg at a time and leave it to hatch by itself. Centipedes hide during the day, under stones, in the soil or under tree bark.

FOOD

Centipedes are fierce meat-eaters. They eat worms, insects, slugs, snails and even lizards. They hunt for food at night.

The centipede's segmented body allows it to bend and twist to help it move through the soil. This female is guarding her eggs.

Chad

See also: Africa

Chad is a large country in central Africa. It has mountains, hills, lowlands and marshes. On the western border is Lake Chad, which used to be very big. Lack of rain during the wet season has made it much smaller.

Living and working

Most people in Chad live in the countryside. The sun-baked houses have thick walls and small windows to keep out the heat.

People in Chad eat meat or fish, served with rice, millet and groundnut sauce. Meat and fish are often grilled. Farmers grow cotton, rice, sorghum and groundnuts. They also herd cattle, sheep and goats. People make fabric out of cotton. Some of the cotton is then sold to other countries.

Grains, dried vegetables and farm animals are sold in open-air markets. There are also stalls selling colourful rugs and brightly patterned leather sandals. This woman is selling flour.

DID YOU KNOW?

In Chad there is a musical instrument called the *hu-hu*. It is made from a bell-shaped hollowed gourd. It can be played like a trumpet or used like a megaphone to make the voice louder.

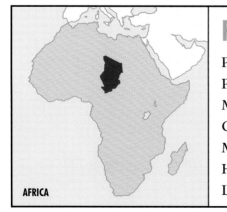

AFRICA

FACT FILE

PEOPLE .... Chadians

POPULATION .... almost 7 million

MAIN LANGUAGES .... Arabic, French, Hausa

CAPITAL CITY .... N'djamena

MONEY .... CFA franc

HIGHEST MOUNTAIN .... Emi Koussi – 3415 m

LONGEST RIVER .... Chari River – 730 km

Cheetah

See also: Cat, Mammal

The cheetah is a member of the cat family. It is a mammal. Cheetahs are found on the grasslands of Africa and Central Asia. The cheetah is the world's fastest running animal. A cheetah can reach speeds of 100 kph.

Cheetah families

Male and female cheetahs live in completely different ways. A female cheetah takes care of her babies, called cubs, until they are about 18 months old. She may have as many as eight cubs in one litter. When they are tiny their mother makes dens for them, moving home every few days. A male cheetah will live separately with a small group of other males, usually his brothers.

CHEETAH FACTS

NUMBER OF KINDS	1
COLOUR	gold with black spots
LENGTH	1.12–1.15 m (without tail)
HEIGHT	70–90 cm
WEIGHT	up to 72 kg
STATUS	endangered
LIFE SPAN	about 12 years
ENEMIES	lions, poachers (illegal hunters) that kill cheetahs for their fur.

Big lungs for breathing help it run very fast

Spotted fur helps the cheetah hide while it hunts

Long legs for speed

A cheetah

FOOD

A cheetah chases and kills animals, such as impalas and hares, to eat them.

A mother cheetah looks after her cubs by herself. The cubs already have their spotted fur.

Chicken

See also: Bird

A chicken is a bird. Chickens are raised all over the world for their meat, feathers and eggs. In the past there were many kinds of wild chicken. Most chickens are now kept by people.

Chicken families

A male chicken is called a cockerel and a female chicken is called a hen. The babies are called chicks. Chickens like to live together in groups, called flocks. A flock can have one or two cockerels and up to 20 hens and their chicks. The hens lay up to ten eggs. They sit on them to keep them warm until the chicks hatch.

On many farms hens live inside, in cages, without cockerels or chicks. They lay eggs onto a moving belt which travels below the cages. These eggs are sent to supermarkets.

CHICKEN FACTS

NUMBER OF MAIN BREEDS	4
COLOUR	most commonly, white, brown or black
WEIGHT	1.5–4 kg
STATUS	common
LIFE SPAN	up to 6 years
ENEMIES	foxes, people

A Rhode Island red

Beak for picking up small bits of food

Fancy tail to show off

Sharp claws to scratch the ground to find food

FOOD

Chickens scratch the soil to find seeds, worms and insects. A hen will catch flies for her chicks. When chickens are kept in cages, the farmer feeds them with pellets made from cereals and vitamins.

Baby chicks peck their way out of their shells.

Chile

See also: South America

Chile is a long, narrow country in South America. It has high mountains in the east and low mountains at the coast. In between, there is a warm valley. In the north there is desert.

Living and working

Many people live in towns in the central valley. A third of the whole population lives in the capital, Santiago. Chile was once ruled by Spain and its buildings, music and dancing are all still very Spanish. There are also many local Indian groups, such as the Arauncans. They have their own traditions, including weaving blankets. The people of Chile like eating spiced meat or cheese pastries called *empanadas*. They also eat a dish made of mashed sweetcorn, called *humitas*.

Farmers raise animals and grow cereals, tomatoes, potatoes and many fruits.

Farmers still travel across the open mountain valleys on horseback to check on their sheep and cattle.

DID YOU KNOW?

The name 'Chile' comes from the word '*tchili*'. This is a word in a local Indian language that means 'snow'.

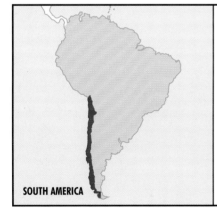

SOUTH AMERICA

FACT FILE

PEOPLE	Chilean
POPULATION	14 million
MAIN LANGUAGE	Spanish
CAPITAL CITY	Santiago
MONEY	Chilean peso
HIGHEST MOUNTAIN	Ojos del Salado – 6880 m
LONGEST RIVER	Loa River – 350 km

China

See also: China (Ancient) Asia

China is the world's third largest country. It is in Asia. The Himalaya Mountains are in the south-west. In the east are warm lowlands. Nearly a quarter of all the people in the world are Chinese.

Living and working

Most Chinese live in the warm lowlands. Three great rivers provide water. People use boats on the rivers to travel around the country. Farmers grow rice in special flooded fields.

China has many large, modern cities. The streets are crowded with bicycles as people travel to and from their work.

The Chinese eat rice or noodles with most meals. They use chopsticks to eat their food. The most important holiday in China is the Chinese New Year. Dancers in dragon costumes parade through the streets, and there are fireworks.

The Great Wall of China is one of the most impressive things people have ever built. It can even be seen from space.

DID YOU KNOW?

The Great Wall of China is over 5000 km long. It was started in 214 BC and took 1000 years to finish.

FACT FILE

PEOPLE	Chinese
POPULATION	1.2 billion
MAIN LANGUAGES	Mandarin Chinese and local languages
CAPITAL CITY	Beijing
LARGEST CITY	Shanghai
MONEY	Yuan
HIGHEST MOUNTAINS	Kunlun range
LONGEST RIVER	Yangtze River – 6380 km

China, Ancient

See also: China

Ancient China lasted from about 1700 BC to AD 1279. It was ruled by different families. Each period of time when a different family ruled is called a dynasty.

What were the Ancient Chinese like?

From 221 BC the Ancient Chinese were ruled by an emperor. Most of the ordinary people were farmers who grew crops in the fields and sold them at markets. The Ancient Chinese believed in spirits that they thought could affect their lives. They also followed the teachings of great thinkers such as Buddha and Confucius.

What are the Ancient Chinese famous for?

The Ancient Chinese are famous for inventing porcelain china, paper, type for printing, the wheelbarrow and gunpowder. They are also famous for making silk and for building the Great Wall of China.

What happened to the Ancient Chinese?

Ancient China was taken over by the Mongols in 1279, but they let the Chinese live the same way as they had before.

KEY DATES

1700 BC.. First Ancient Chinese dynasty, the Shang, set up

770 BC.... Zhou dynasty ends. Families fight to rule China

221 BC.... Shi Huangdi takes over all China. He calls himself the First Emperor

AD 1279.. The Mongols invade. The Ancient Chinese empire falls

Emperor Shi Huangdi had this terracotta army buried with him to defend him in the afterlife. The figures are over 2000 years old. Each figure is slightly different.

Christianity

See also: Cathedral

Christianity is a world religion. Its followers are called Christians. The religion grew from the teachings of Jesus Christ. Christians believe that Jesus was the son of God.

This Christian service is being held outdoors in South Africa.

The life of Jesus Christ

Jesus was born in Palestine about 2000 years ago. He was a Jewish carpenter who also became a famous preacher. People travelled long distances to hear him talk about how they could change their lives. Government and religious leaders worried about people following Jesus. He was sentenced to death by crucifixion.

Beliefs and teachings

The followers of Jesus believed that after he died, he rose again from the dead. They started spreading his teachings. This was the beginning of the new religion called Christianity. The New Testament in the Bible tells the story of Jesus and his teachings.

Christianity today

There are now about 1.7 billion Christians all over the world. Christians worship at home and in churches. The most important Christian festival is Easter, which celebrates Jesus' death and rebirth.

This modern Christian church in California is called the Crystal Cathedral.

Classical music

See also: Music, Musical instruments, Orchestra

Classical music is music written for groups of instruments, such as orchestras. It can also be for singers.

The first classical music

Before classical music, most music was played on single instruments. It was also sung or chanted in churches and cathedrals.

Classical music began in Europe in the fifteenth century. Composers, or music writers, started writing down music for bigger and bigger groups of instruments.

Rulers and nobles would pay to have music written and performed especially for them. Later, people started music colleges which taught classical music. Concerts of classical music were performed in public places, so anyone who wanted to listen could go.

Johann Sebastian Bach (1685–1750)

Bach is a very famous German composer. He came from a musical family. He played the violin and viola. He wrote music for groups of instruments, for the organ and for singers. One of his most famous pieces is the B Minor Mass.

TYPES OF CLASSICAL MUSIC

Symphony....... A long piece of music written for a big group of musicians playing in an orchestra

Concerto.......... A piece of music written for an orchestra. One instrument plays the most important part

Chamber music............... Music written for a small orchestra, or an even smaller groups

Opera............. A play set to music, with an orchestra and a chorus of singers. Special singers called soloists act and sing the important parts

Choral music... Music for a group of singers. There may also be an orchestra or some instruments playing with them

This small orchestra is playing chamber music.

Climate

See also: Season, Weather

The climate of a region is the pattern of heat, wind and rain there. The day-to-day change in climate in a region is called the weather.

Climate and seasons

Most places in the world have a pattern of weather during the year. This pattern breaks the year into parts called seasons. The types of seasons in a region decide its climate.

Six climate regions

1 **Polar regions** – These areas are very cold all year round. There is permanent snow and ice.

2 **Cold regions** – These areas have a spring and summer but they are very short and it never gets very warm.

3 **Cold temperate regions** – These areas have four seasons, with a cold winter and a warm summer.

4 **Warm temperate regions** – These areas have four seasons, but the summer is very hot and the winter doesn't get very cold.

5 **Dry regions** – All of the world's deserts are dry regions. There is very little or no rain.

6 **Tropical regions** – These areas have heavy rain throughout the year.

The Earth's climate regions

Coast

See also: Bay, Delta, Ocean, Peninsula

The coast is where the land meets the sea. The edge of the land is called the coastline. Some coasts have steep cliffs where mountains come down into the sea. Others have wide beaches with flat land behind them. Coastlines may have bays or rivers running into the sea.

How coasts change

The coastline is always changing. Waves wear away some parts of a coast. Waves and currents wash pieces of rock along the coast. Over many thousands of years, some of these pieces may be broken up very small and washed ashore. This is how a beach is made.

The coastline in this picture is being worn away by the sea. This is called erosion. Some buildings have fallen into the sea.

People and the coast

Sometimes the sea is so rough that the coastline is washed away, taking roads and houses with it. Where this happens, people build special concrete and stone walls to protect the coast. Other coasts are used by tourists and local people for swimming and boating. Countries with coasts often have big fishing industries. There may also be large harbours where ships come to load and unload goods.

This coastline is partly high chalk cliffs that go down directly into the sea, and partly a rocky coast.

Cockroach

See also: Insect

A cockroach is an insect. In some places it is a well-known household pest. Most cockroaches, however, live outdoors in hot, tropical countries.

Cockroach families

The female cockroach lays her eggs in a tough egg case. The eggs hatch into nymphs. A nymph looks like an adult, but it has no wings. Cockroaches like to hide in houses, in walls, cupboards and other small spaces. Outside, they hide under stones, logs and bark, or in ant and termite nests.

COCKROACH FACTS

NUMBER OF KINDS	3500
COLOUR	usually black or brown
LENGTH	up to 10 cm
STATUS	common
LIFE SPAN	about 2.5 years
ENEMIES	people, spiders, birds

FOOD

The cockroach is a scavenger that feeds at night on any food and water it can find. In a house, dirty plates, pet food and spilt food in cupboards all attract cockroaches.

Thick, leathery skin for protection

Long antennae to smell food

An American cockroach

Hairs on its legs touch and feel things

This female giant burrowing cockroach is with her nymphs. Cockroaches have spread almost everywhere, carried with goods in aircraft, ships and trains.

Colombia

See also: South America

Colombia is a country in South America. The Andes Mountains run from north to south through Colombia. In the east are grassy, flat lands and rainforests.

Living and working

Most Colombians live in the cities. The cities are crowded with buses and cars. People sell sweets and fruit on the street. In the countryside there are big farms where people work growing coffee and sugar. Ordinary farmers have very little land. It is hard for them to make enough money to live.

Colombians grow and eat a lot of maize. They make it into soups, stews and drinks. They also make flat pancakes called tortillas from ground maize flour.

DID YOU KNOW?

Most of the emeralds used in jewellery come from Colombia.

One of Colombia's largest crops is coffee. Here coffee beans are being picked off coffee bushes.

SOUTH AMERICA

FACT FILE

PEOPLE .... Colombians
POPULATION .... 34 million
MAIN LANGUAGE .... Spanish
CAPITAL CITY .... Bogotá
MONEY .... Colombian peso
HIGHEST MOUNTAIN .... Pico Cristóbal Colón – 5775 m
LONGEST RIVER .... Magdalena River – 1600 km

Colour

See also: Light, Television

Colour is seen when light is reflected off an object and bounces into the eyes of the person looking at it. The colour of an object depends on the light that it reflects.

Different colours

When using coloured paint or ink, there are three main or primary colours. These are red, blue and yellow. Any other colour can be made by mixing these three colours together. When all the colours are blended together, the result is almost black.

When coloured lights are blended, the three primary lights are red, blue and green. Light of any other colour can be made by mixing the three primary lights.

The pictures on a television screen are all made up of tiny dots of red, blue and green light. When all the colours are blended together, they make white light.

Using colour

Colour can be used in signals, for instance in red flags or traffic lights. They can be used to warn of danger. Animals also use colour. They can use it to attract a mate, to scare away enemies or to hide.

DID YOU KNOW?

Black and white are not real colours. An object looks white when it reflects all the light that falls on it. An object looks black when it does not reflect any of the light.

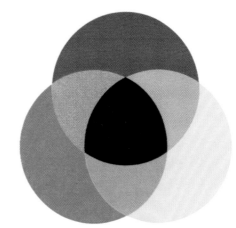

This colour wheel shows how coloured paints or inks can be blended to make different colours.

The red, yellow and green colours used in traffic lights are well-known signals.

Comet

See also: Meteor, Planet, Solar system, Sun

A comet is a giant ball of ice, dust, gases and rock. It looks like a star with a glowing tail. Comets can only be seen as they get close to the sun.

What makes a comet?

There are many comets in our solar system. Most are far from the sun. In the cold of outer space they stay frozen. Each year, a few comets are pulled closer to the sun. As a comet gets closer to the sun it gets hotter and starts to boil away. This makes the comet's long tail.

Most comets can only be seen through a telescope. If a comet is very bright it can be seen in the sky at night.

Halley's comet is seen every 76 years. It will next be seen in 2062 AD.

A comet's journey

Some comets travel around the sun in a special path called an orbit. It takes the comet a fixed number of years to complete each orbit.

DID YOU KNOW?

Halley's Comet is seen from the Earth every 76 years. It is named after the English astronomer Edmond Halley. He first saw it in 1682 and worked out when it would be seen next.

This is the Hale/Bopp comet, seen from Earth in 1997. The blue tail is made up of gas from the comet head. The white tail is made of dust, also from the comet head.

Communication

See also: Computer, Internet, Radio, Telephone, Television

Communication means sending messages. The messages can be information, ideas or feelings. Speaking and writing are types of communication, and so is the expression on a person's face.

Changes in communication

For a long time, letters were the only way to send private messages. In 1844 the telegraph system was first used. It sent electric messages along wires, using Morse code. Then, in 1876, Alexander Graham Bell invented the telephone. Today fax and e-mail messages are sent along telephone wires.

Radio communication was invented in 1895. Signals move through the air and don't need wires. Television made it possible to send moving pictures by radio signals.

This modern communications centre uses telephones, special headsets and computers.

Light can now be used to send messages along special wires called optical fibres. Thousands of messages can go along each fibre. Cable TV systems uses optical cables.

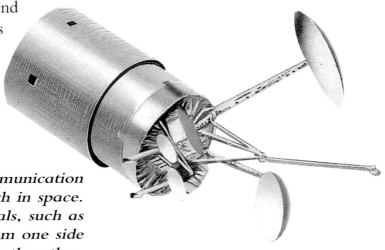

Satellites, like this communication satellite, circle the Earth in space. They bounce signals, such as telephone calls, from one side of the Earth to the other.

Computer

See also: Bar code, Laser

A computer is a machine that can deal with information very quickly. Many things, such as cars and washing machines, are controlled by tiny computers.

The first computers

The first computer was built by Charles Babbage in England, in 1833. ENIAC, the first electronic computer, was built in the United States, in 1946. It was as big as a small house.

Smaller and better

As electronics got better, the parts could be made smaller and more powerful. The microchip, made in the 1960s, could do the job of many of the large computer circuits.

The first personal computer, for people to use at home, was made in about 1975. These desktop computers were about as powerful as the huge ENIAC. Today, computers keep getting smaller, faster and more powerful.

A personal computer

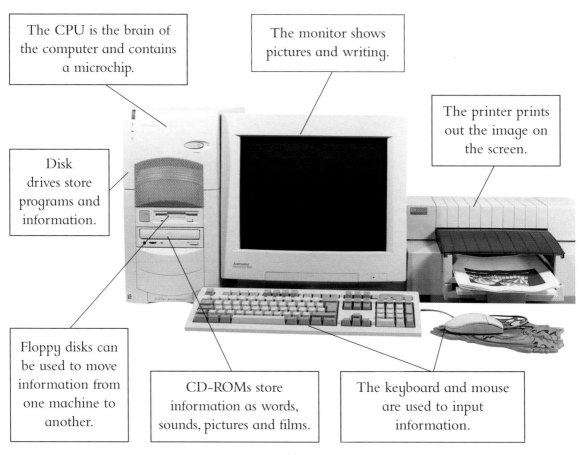

The CPU is the brain of the computer and contains a microchip.

The monitor shows pictures and writing.

The printer prints out the image on the screen.

Disk drives store programs and information.

Floppy disks can be used to move information from one machine to another.

CD-ROMs store information as words, sounds, pictures and films.

The keyboard and mouse are used to input information.

Continent

See also: Earth, Ocean

A continent is a very large area of land. There are seven continents in the world. People called geologists study what the continents are made up of, and how they formed.

On the move

Continents have not always been where they are now. Millions of years ago there was just one big piece of land. Over time, this land has split and the continents have moved apart. The continents are still moving about 2 cm each year.

HOW MUCH LAND?

ASIA	45 million sq km
AFRICA	30.2 million sq km
NORTH AMERICA	24.9 million sq km
SOUTH AMERICA	17.8 million sq km
ANTARCTICA	13.2 million sq km
EUROPE	10.5 million sq km
AUSTRALASIA	7.7 million sq km

HOW MANY PEOPLE?

ASIA	3 billion
EUROPE	728 million
AFRICA	648 million
NORTH AMERICA	395 million
SOUTH AMERICA	285 million
AUSTRALASIA	27 million
ANTARCTICA	no permanent residents

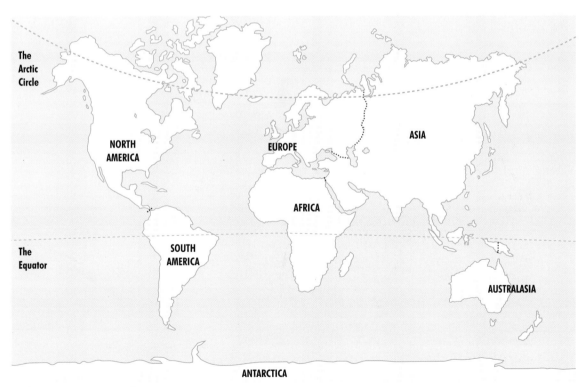

The Arctic Circle

NORTH AMERICA

EUROPE

ASIA

AFRICA

The Equator

SOUTH AMERICA

AUSTRALASIA

ANTARCTICA

The seven continents

Coral

See also: Coast, Island

Coral is made up of the skeletons of millions of tiny animals called polyps. Coral forms in shallow, tropical seas. Whole islands can be made out of coral. Some large stretches of coral are called reefs. The Great Barrier Reef in Australia is made from coral.

Coral reef

A coral reef is made when living polyps attach themselves to existing coral. Some polyps hatch from eggs produced by adults. Others form as buds on polyps that have already grown. Each new polyp settles on the reef and makes its own stony skeleton for protection. When one polyp dies, new polyps build on top of it. The coral reef gradually grows larger.

CORAL FACTS

NUMBER OF KINDS	2300
COLOUR	orange, yellow, brown, purple, green
LENGTH OF A SINGLE POLYP	2.5–30 cm
LENGTH OF A CORAL REEF	up to 2010 km
STATUS	common
REEF LIFE SPAN	thousands to millions of years
ENEMIES	people, other sea animals

A stony coral polyp

This new polyp hasn't yet built a stony skeleton around itself.

FOOD

A coral polyp feeds at night on floating larvae. Stinging tentacles trap food that drifts into their grasp. Tiny plants that live inside each polyp's body also make food that the polyp eats.

Some corals look like trees, others look like fans or pipes. This coral is part of the Great Barrier Reef in Australia.